Portrait of
Scotland

First published in Great Britain in 1997 for Lomond Books
36 West Shore Road, Granton
Edinburgh EH5 1QD

Produced by Colin Baxter Photography Ltd.

Reprinted 1999, 2002, 2003
First published in paperback in 2005

A CIP catalogue record for this book is available from the British Library

ISBN 1-84204-077-4

Printed in China

Front Cover Photograph: Ben Lomond and Loch Ard, Trossachs.
Back Cover Photograph: Loch Duich and the Kintail Mountains.
Page One Photograph: Loch Linnhe.

Portrait of
Scotland

Photographs by Colin Baxter

LOMOND

Contents

Culduie, Wester Ross (left); Loch Lomond from the slopes of Ben Lomond (following page).

Introduction

How can you capture a portrait of Scotland on film? Only by travelling its length and breadth in every season. Scotland offers a variety of landscape and light out of all proportion to its size. Its story grows out of the very rocks of which it is made — from the gouging of glaciers in the not-so-long ago Ice Age, to the rock cuttings made for modern Highland roads. Its history and land use can be read wherever you travel in the countryside.

There are contrasts at every turn. What could be more different in texture than the cool grey glint of Grampian granite from the warm honey sandstone of Edinburgh? Or the red blocks which build Orkney's cliffs from the pale quartz screes which stream off the ancient eroded peaks of the far north-west? And if the very building blocks of Scotland are so characteristic, then the landscapes they support reflect this, from the Southern Uplands' lush river-valley woodlands to the endless boggy moors of Caithness.

Rock, wood, pasture and moor are overlaid with a pattern of land use which tells both of Scotland's past and its present. The ruins of ancient castles are the most obvious signs of a martial story. But there are also more subtle signs to look for, from the faint stripes of the lazy-beds of a long-vanished rural Highland population to the random, marbled pattern of an eastern Highland grouse moor after years of annual heather burning.

There are few other places where such a sense of continuity is woven into the landscape. The Scots pines, with their open understorey of juniper and blaeberry, surviving in places like Rothiemurchus below the Cairngorms, are the descendants of trees which sheltered bear and elk. The western seaboard, where the horizon-profiles of far-flung islands alternately dissolve and re-appear as the Atlantic squalls pass over, looks the same now as it did when the Viking raiders and traders named the high peaks of the island of Rum.

Rock forms, land use and a sense of permanency are only some of the elements in the portrait. Yet another factor is plain from a glimpse of a map of Europe. Scotland is a tiny country, up at the bows of the Continent, butting into the north Atlantic. On one side are the mild but moist weather patterns sailing in from the south-west. (This is why the lushest and most exotic gardens are in the west, while many eastern extremities of Scotland get less rain than, say, Rome.) The high pressure and more stable systems of the Continent lie out to the east. Where do the two weather systems, ocean and continental, meet? Somewhere in the Minch perhaps today, or the central corridor around Stirling tomorrow, or the Border hills next week.

Ever-changing, hour upon hour, the weather fronts battle it out over the heads of the Scottish folk. They accept both the warm gold of the late summer after harvest and the cold silver of the Arctic blast, when clear northern air brings into sharp focus mountains sixty miles away (and more) from the viewer. In Scotland, the quality of light owes everything to this essential instability of the weather. It creates the palette of rainbows and haloes, orange tints, rain-washed greens, piercing blues and diffuse yellows which paints the landscapes as the year – or as the day – goes round.

However, we did not always appreciate this wonderfully visual element in the Scottish landscape. For most of the 18th century, for example, the wilderness of the northlands was seen as a decidedly unromantic and fearful place of savagery. Later, Sir Walter Scott helped change the perception of Scotland, creating a mix of the sentimental and the grand in his verse-narratives and novels. Before him, the cult of the picturesque had already taken root in the Romantic Age, with Coleridge and Wordsworth just two of the Romantic poets who ventured beyond the Highland line in the early 19th century. By that time, the first real tourists had already journeyed north in search of the perfect Scottish picture, which they composed in a suitably framed mirror, their 'viewing glass', which it was the fashion to carry with them.

Painters, too, came to interpret Scotland in a dramatic light, both as visitors, such as JMW Turner, and as natives, like the Reverend John Thomson – a kind of Sir Walter Scott in paint – or Horatio McCulloch with his gloomy crags and castles like scaled-up picture postcards. In the 19th century, they all responded emotionally to the austere and unforgiving landscapes of Highland Scotland, and influenced the way we perceive the place today.

Yet any portrait of Scotland cannot be exclusively Highland. Another angle is represented by, say, the fishing villages of Fife, with their long struggle with the sea and their architecture which speaks of ancient trading links with the Low Countries. The wooded river valleys and pastoral scenes of the Scottish Borders also contribute to the picture. Essential Scotland also has to encompass the liveliness of its cities: the style and panache of Glasgow or the sheer theatricality of Edinburgh. Industrial Scotland even has its own icon in the shape of the Forth Rail Bridge, the epitome of Victorian confidence and exuberance, and also a symbol in steel of the grandeur and drama of Scotland.

The islands, too, have much to add to a complex and many-faceted picture. Those of the Clyde estuary, such as Arran, have for generations played a part as an escape from the industry of the central corridor of Scotland. Generations of Glaswegians, for instance, have trampled the granite ridges of Goat Fell — or at least enjoyed the view of its distinctive profile from the ferry.

Further to the west, the Inner Hebrides beckon with all their varied charms: Islay of the glorious beaches, yet a place busy with whisky distilleries; Mull with its grand castles and pastel-painted Tobermory; or Iona, Mull's tiny neighbour, a place of pilgrimage exerting a pull on thousands of visitors each year out of all proportion to its size. On Colonsay, moor and pasture, woodland, beach and cliff are just the right scale for the near-perfect Hebridean island — irresistibly beguiling. Others might argue that it is further out still, somewhere in the long chain of the Western Isles, that the stronghold of Gaelic culture is to be found.

Not all of Scotland's islands belong to the Celtic world. Orkney and Shetland embrace a Norse heritage. Orkney's cluster of islands has a greater concentration of prehistoric sites than anywhere else in Europe. At Skara Brae you can glimpse the everyday life of the Orcadians' ancient ancestors — a neolithic village, complete with stone furniture. Beyond the horizon, beyond the Viking stepping-stone of Fair Isle, Shetland is positively un-Scottish, so near the surface lie its Norse roots.

Yet the traveller need not voyage so far. Some of Scotland's finest landscapes can be seen almost from the roadside at places like Glencoe or Torridon and many other points in the West Highlands. The light that bathes the hills has a special quality, making the heart ache with its sheer unexpectedness and clarity and adding atmosphere and drama. Its effect can be equally transforming on other rural and urban landscapes, inviting the observer familiar with these scenes to look at them afresh. Small wonder the Romantic poets, the painters and generations of ordinary folk have been inspired by it.

Yes, Scotland really does look like these photographs. This is one man's portrait of the country, capturing its essence in the fleeting moments of light on the elements of rock and water — austere, grand, inspiring or, more likely, something beyond words.

Gilbert Summers

The Highlands and Islands

Loch Torridon, Wester Ross — looking west towards Liathach (left) and from Beinn Alligin (above).

Loch Hourn and Knoydart with Eigg and Rum in the background.

Skye and Raasay from near Applecross.

An Teallach and Strath Beag, Wester Ross.

Loch Ewe, Wester Ross.

'The Three Sisters', Glencoe.

Castle Stalker, Loch Linnhe and Kingairloch.

The Isle of Skye across Inner Sound.

Shieldaig, Wester Ross.

Strath Croe and the mountains of Kintail.

Nostie Post Office, Kyle, Wester Ross.

Summer Isles.

Stac Polly, Wester Ross.

Plockton and Loch Carron.

Beinn Sgritheall and Loch Hourn.

The remote islands of St Kilda — Boreray and stacs (left), Hirta and Dùn (above).

Inverness and the River Ness.

Urquhart Castle and Loch Ness.

Quiraing, Isle of Skye.

The Cuillin Hills and Loch Scavaig, Isle of Skye.

The distinctive profile of the Island of
Rum seen from the golden sands of
Lòn Liath near Arisaig, Lochaber.

Eigg from Arisaig, Lochaber.

Tràigh Scarasta and Chaipaval, Harris.

Loch Druidibeg and Hecla, South Uist.

Ben-Damph and Loch Torridon, Wester Ross.

Vibrant golden colours at
the end of a rainbow near Alligin Shuas,
Upper Loch Torridon, Wester Ross.

Glen Affric and Loch Affric
– from the air with Beinn Fhada in the
distance (left), and in the last light of
late autumn (right).

Argyll and the West

Iona – looking across the Sound of Iona towards Loch Scridain and the Isle of Mull (left);
Iona Abbey bathed in the warm light of a November afternoon (above).

Inveraray Castle, Argyll.

Tarbert harbour, by Loch Fyne, Argyll.

Bridges over the River Clyde, Glasgow.

The warm sandstone colours of Glasgow's tenement buildings alongside Great Western Road, seen from the air.

The Islands of Gometra, Staffa and Iona.

Tobermory, Isle of Mull.

The islands and shore of Loch Lomond in winter.

Loch Lomond from the air.

Oban harbour (above); Bàgh an Tigh-Stòir, Craignish, Argyll (right).

Eastern Scotland and the Borders

Glamis Castle, Angus (left); St Cyrus, near Montrose (above).

Quothquan Law, South Lanarkshire.

Devonshaw Hill and the Upper Clyde Valley, South Lanarkshire.

The Bass Rock near North Berwick.

East Lothian and the Firth of Forth.

Jedburgh Abbey at dusk, Borders.

The Tweed Valley, Borders.

The Old Town and St Giles' Cathedral, Edinburgh.

Edinburgh City Centre and Arthur's Seat from the west.

Pittenweem, Fife (above); The Forth Bridge at dawn (right).

The Grampians and North East

Lochnagar and Balmoral Castle, Deeside (left); Fyvie Castle, Aberdeenshire (above).

A frosty morning near Nethybridge, Strathspey.

Morning mist in November across
Corriechuille near Grantown-on-Spey, with
the great bulk of the Cairngorm mountains
towering in the distance.

Loch Tummel and Schiehallion from the Queen's View.

Loch Laidon, Rannoch Moor.

Loch an Eilein, Rothiemurchus, Strathspey.

The River Spey and Loch Insh, Strathspey.

Aberdeen Town House clock tower at dusk.

Aberdeen harbour and city.

The Cairngorm Mountains from the air.

Remnant Caledonian pine forest
dwarfed below the Cairngorm mountains
at Rothiemurchus, shielding the still waters
of Loch an Eilein.

Loch Tay, Perthshire.

The Falls of Dochart at Killin.

Glen Feshie, Cairngorms.

Looking south from Beinn Mheadhoin high in the Cairngorm mountains.

Glen Avon, near Tomintoul, Moray.

Corgarff Castle, Aberdeenshire.

The Lairig Ghru, Cairngorms, from the air (above), and from near Aviemore (right).

Northern Landscapes

Ardvreck Castle and Loch Assynt, Sutherland (left); Balnakeil Bay, Sutherland (above).

Gaada Stack, Foula, Shetland.

Coppa Wick near Sandness on the west mainland of Shetland – the island of Papa Stour beyond.

Handa Island and Point of Stoer, Sutherland.

Looking north from Handa towards the far north west corner of Sutherland – Cape Wrath.

Ben Hope and Loch Hope, Sutherland.

Foinaven from Oldshoremore, Sutherland.

'The Old Man of Hoy', Orkney.

The prehistoric village of Skara Brae, Orkney.

The northern landscape of Shetland – Breakon, Yell (above); Aith Voe, Mainland (right).

Index of Places